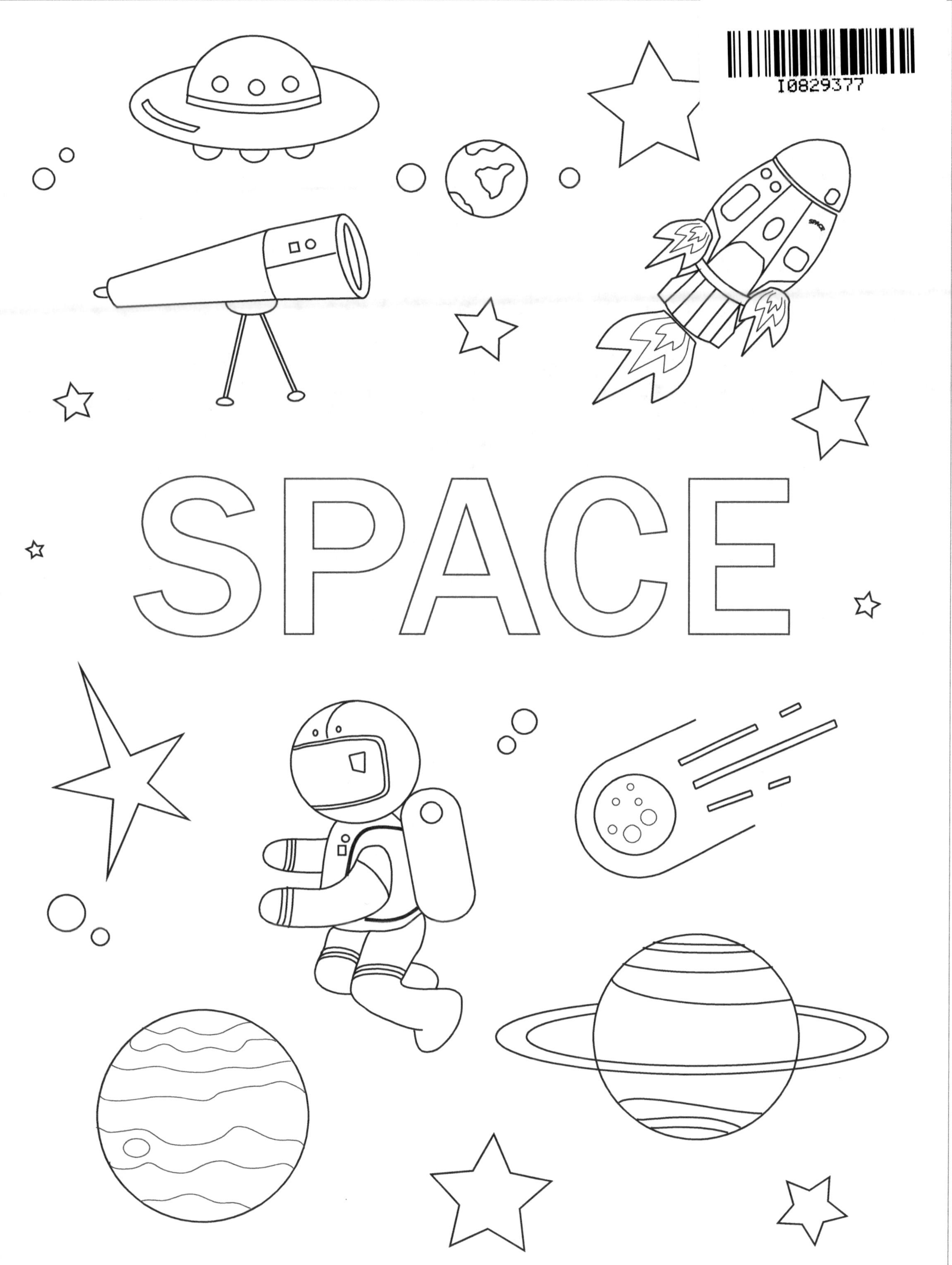

SPACE
I0829377

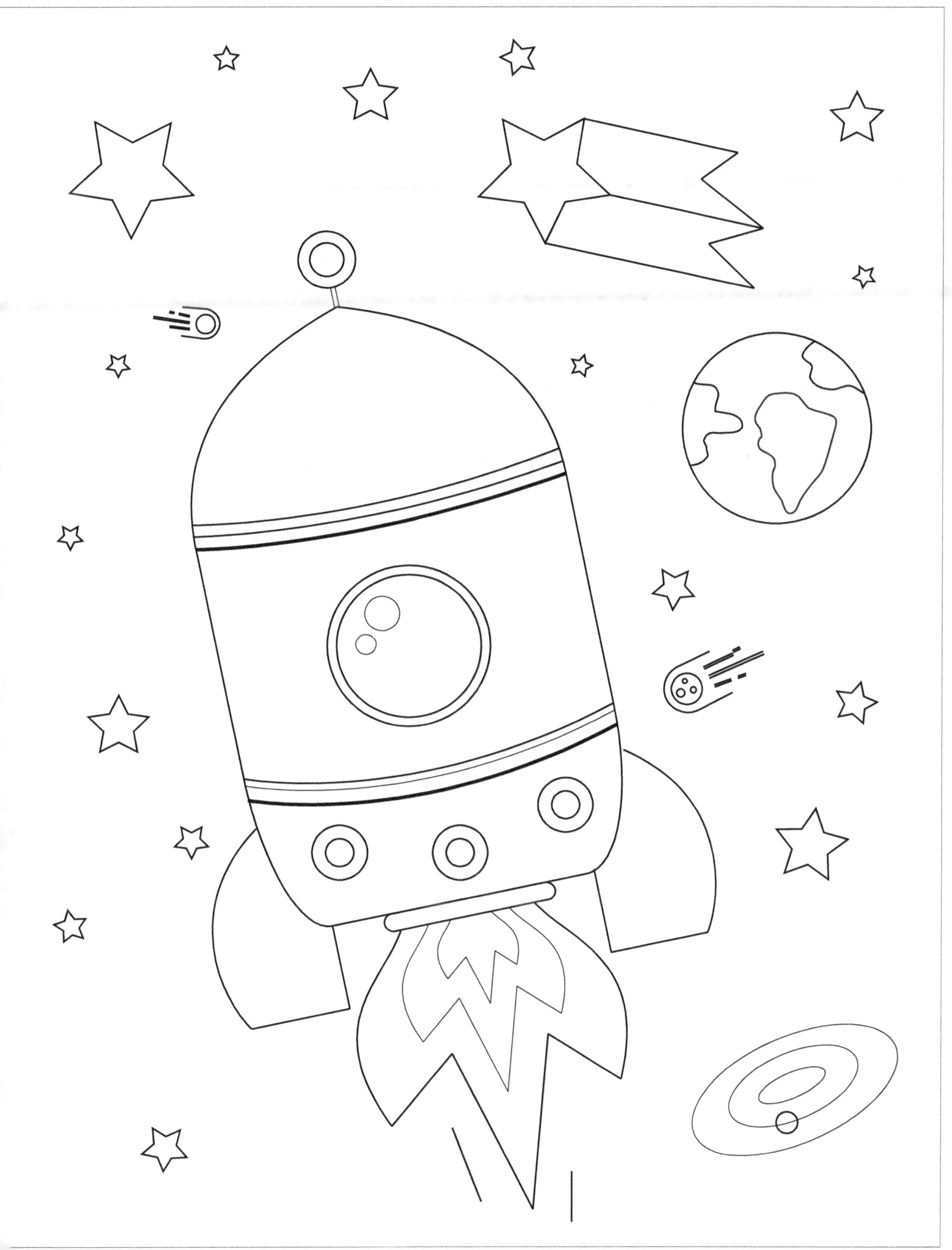

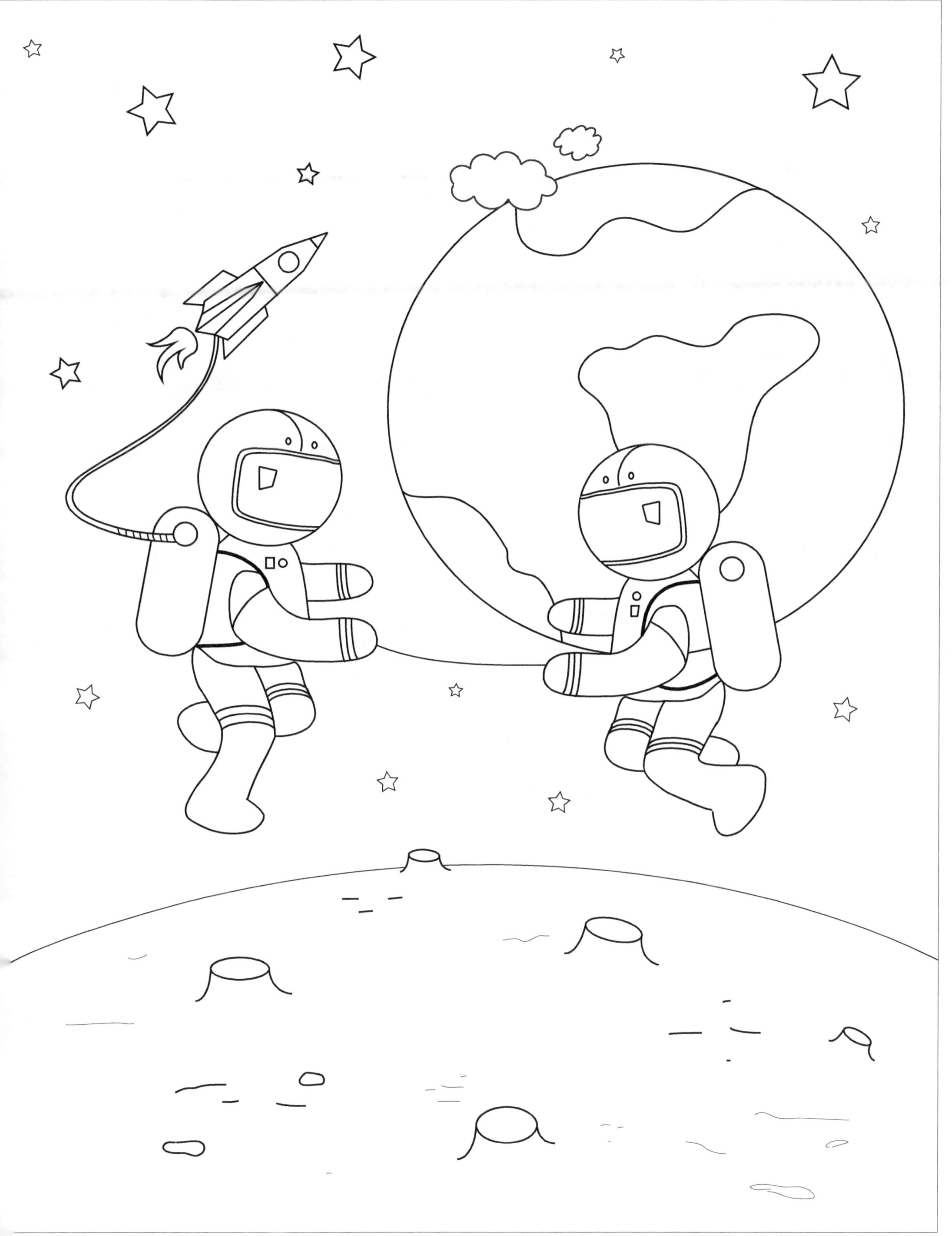

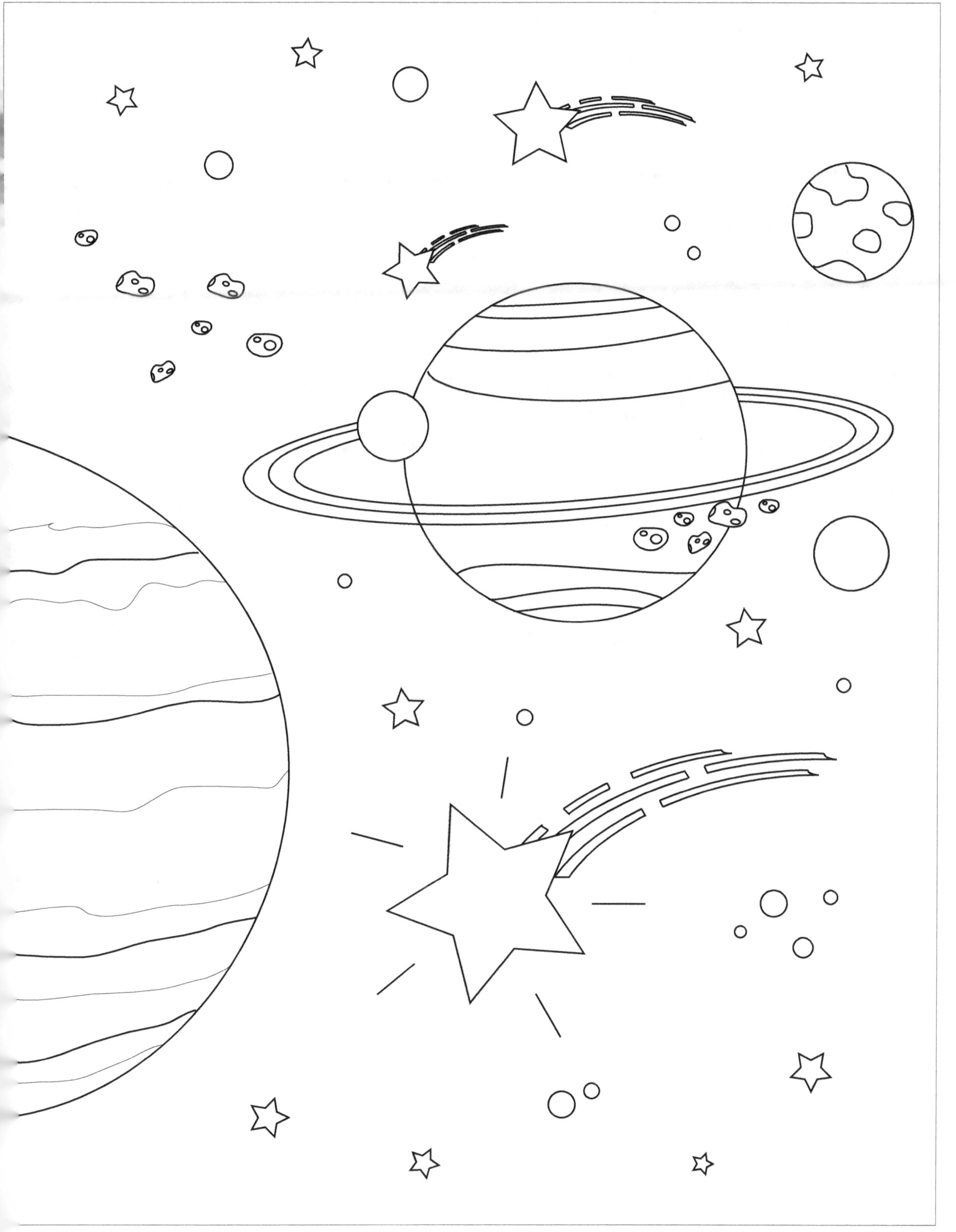

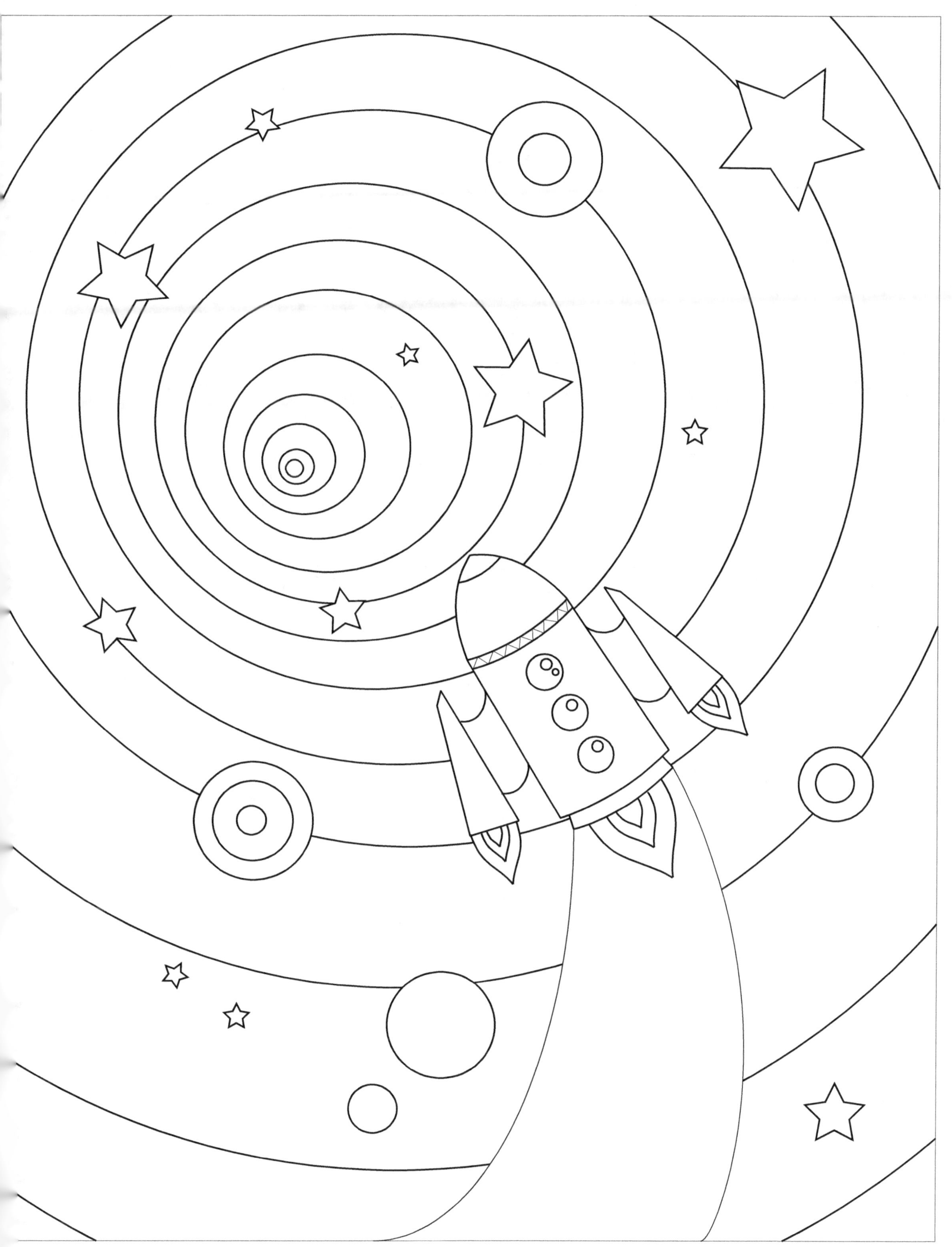

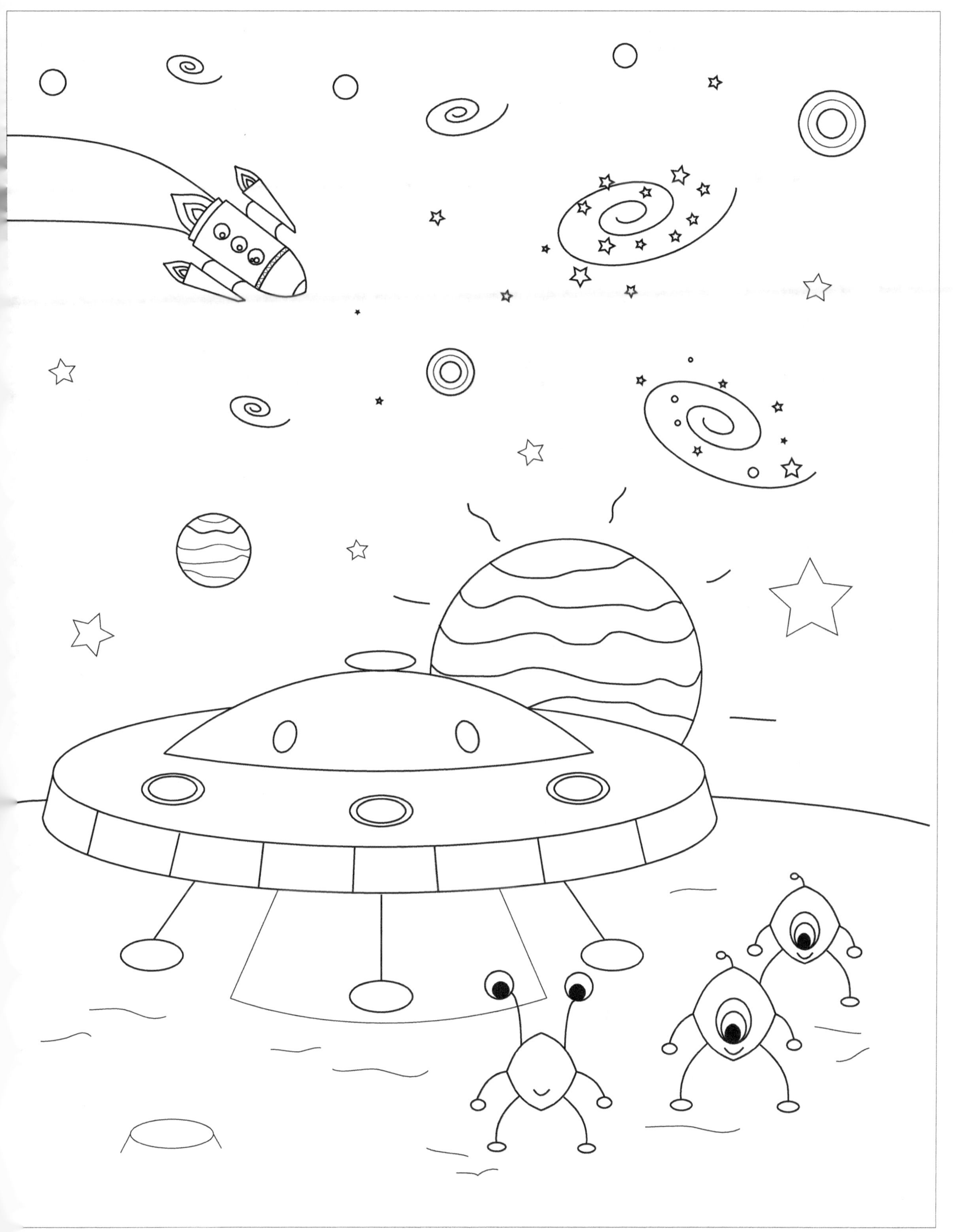

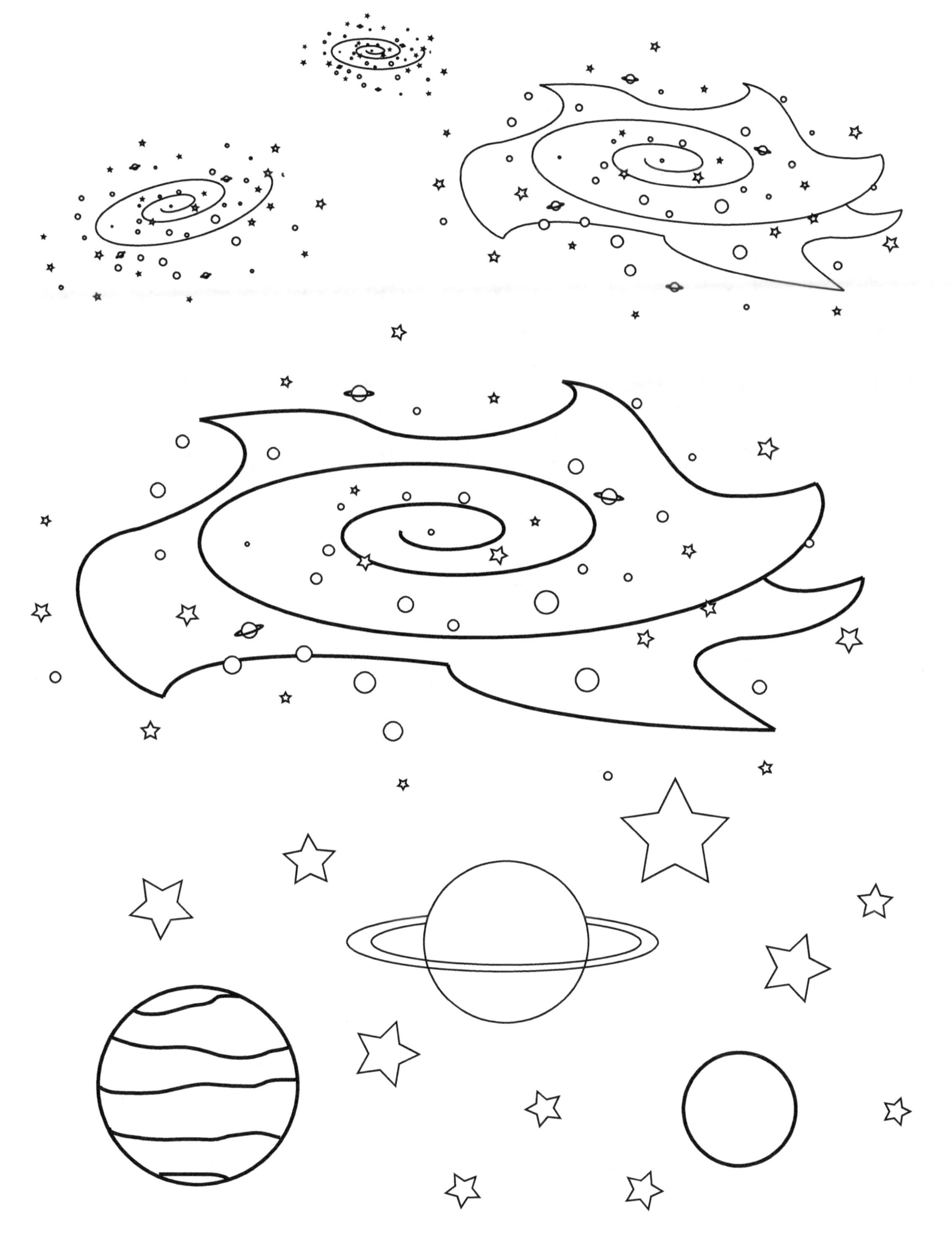

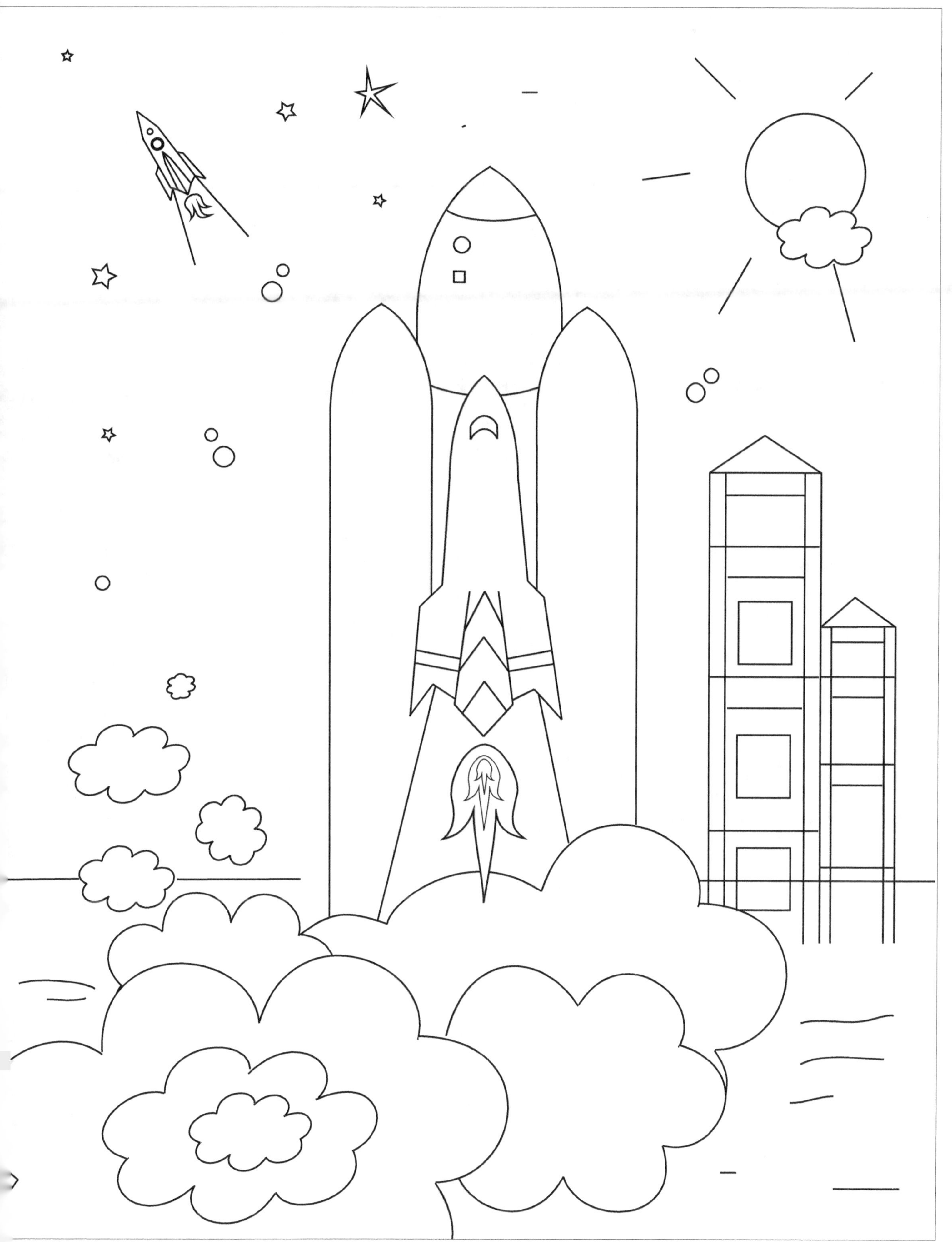

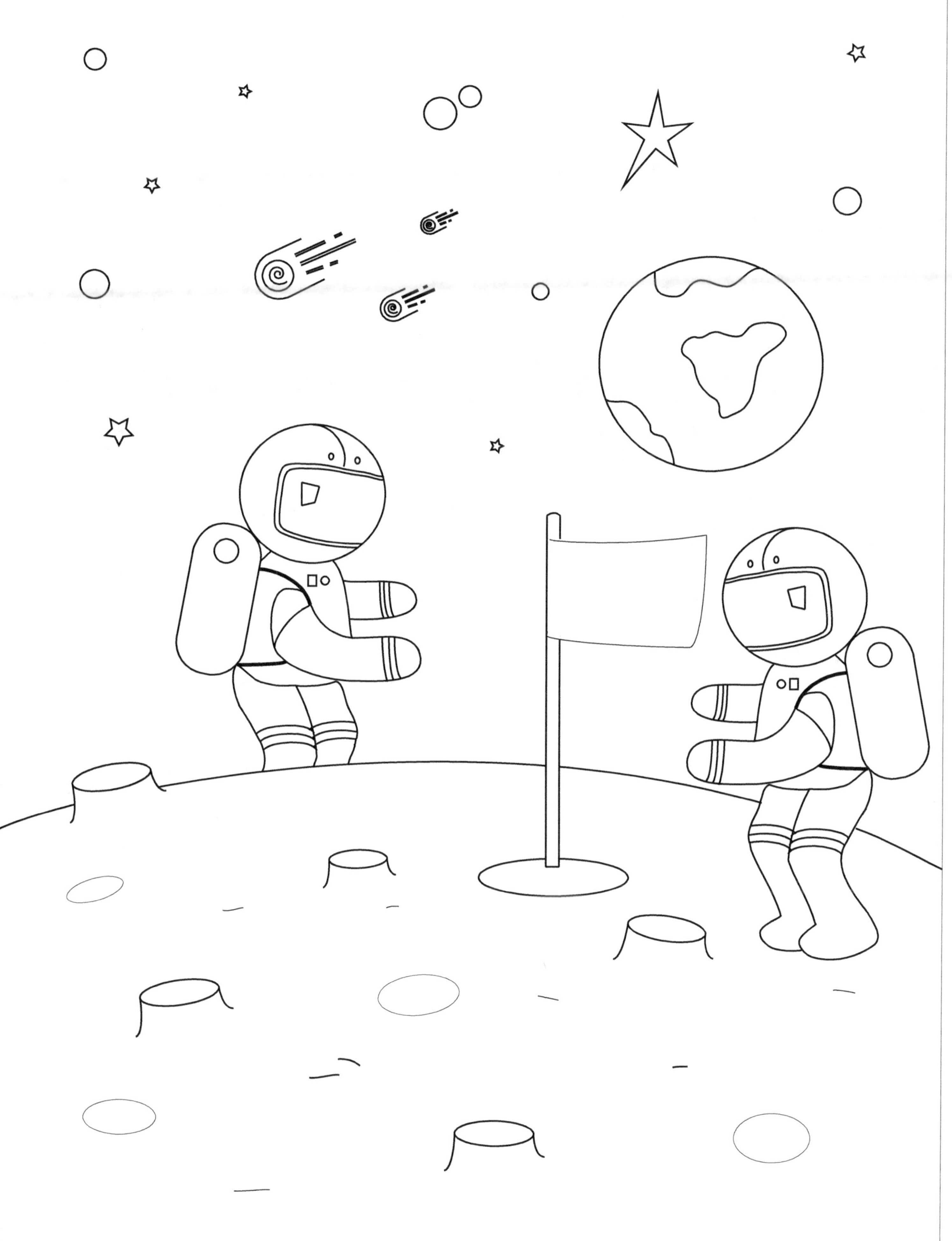

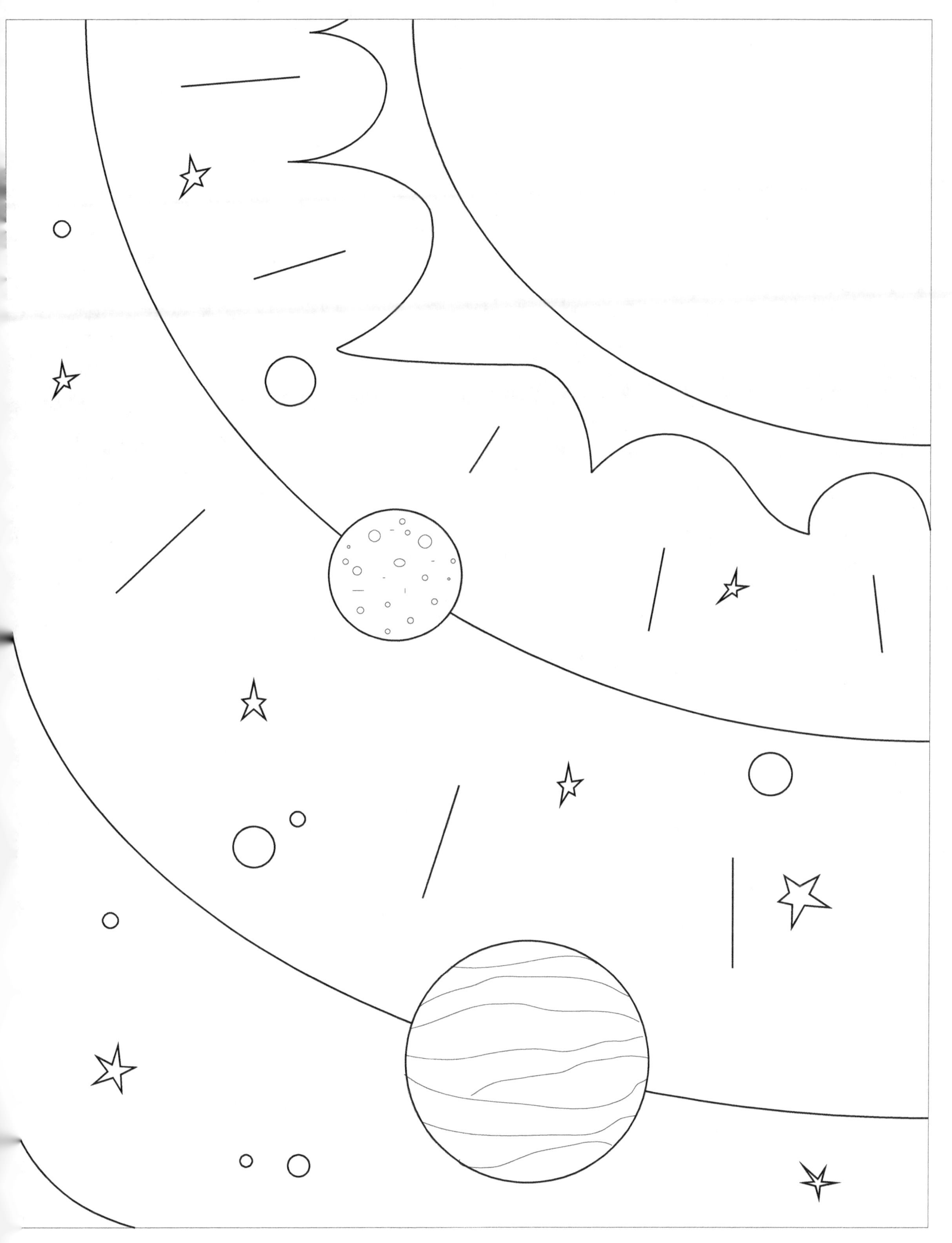

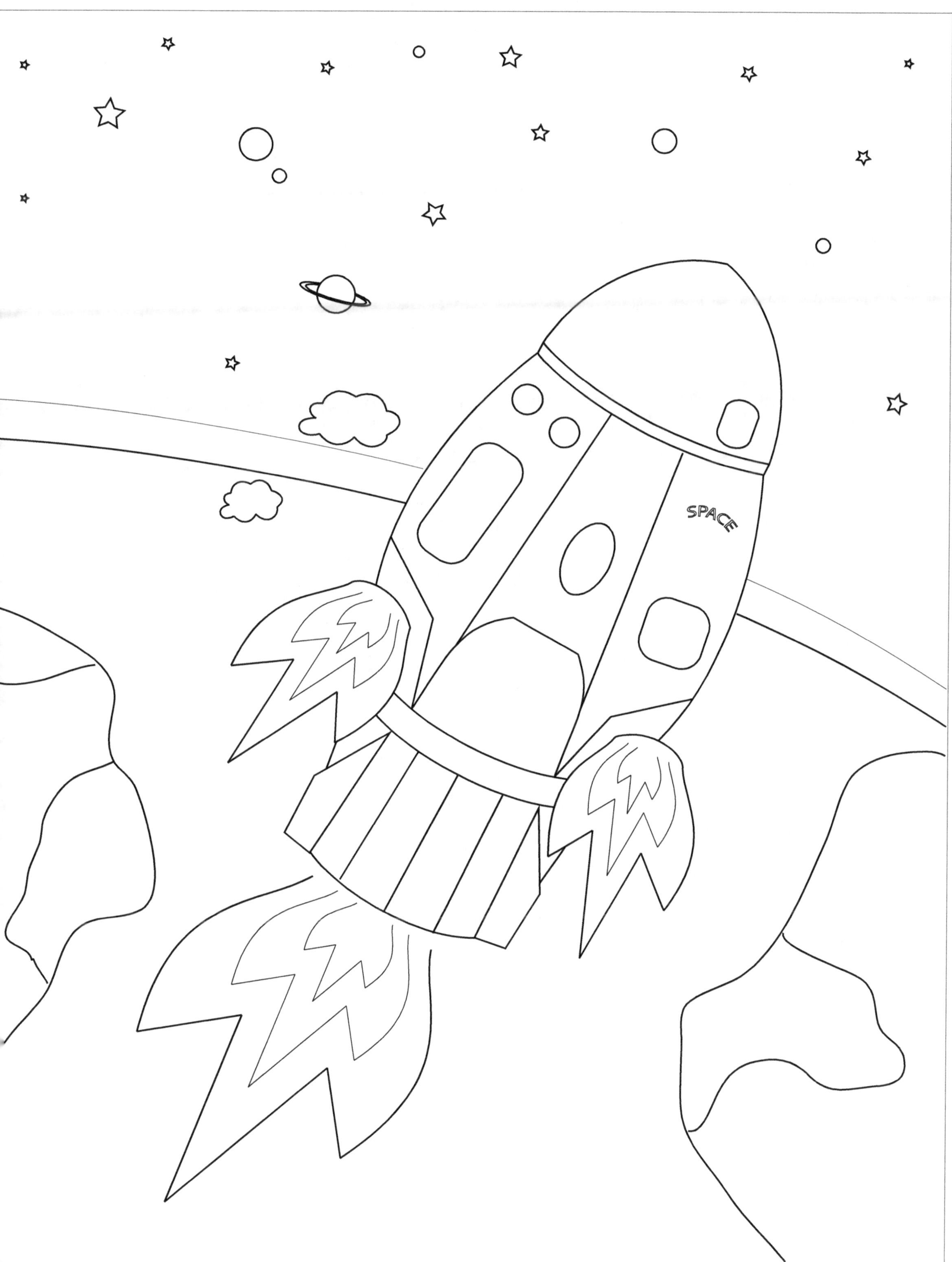
SPACE

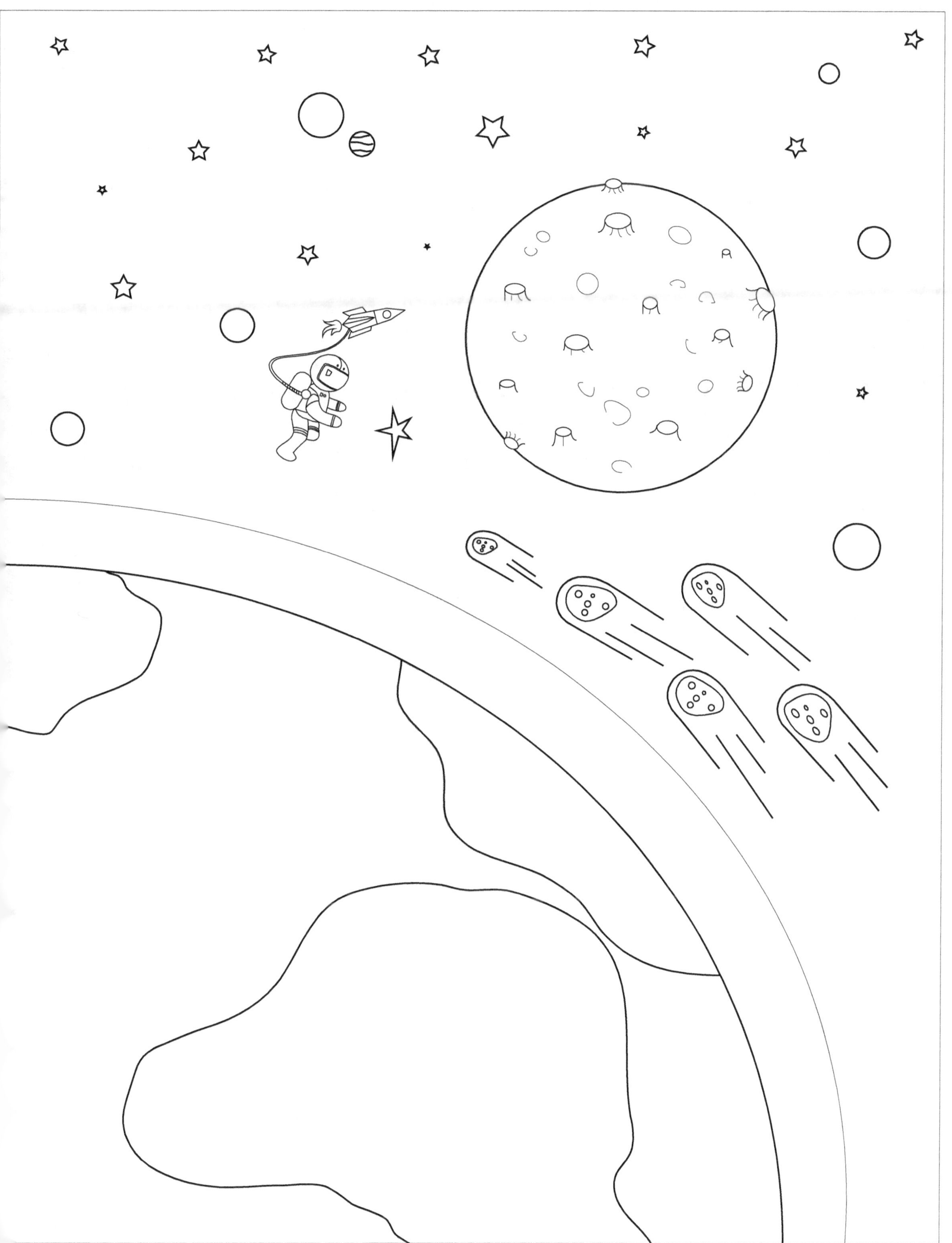

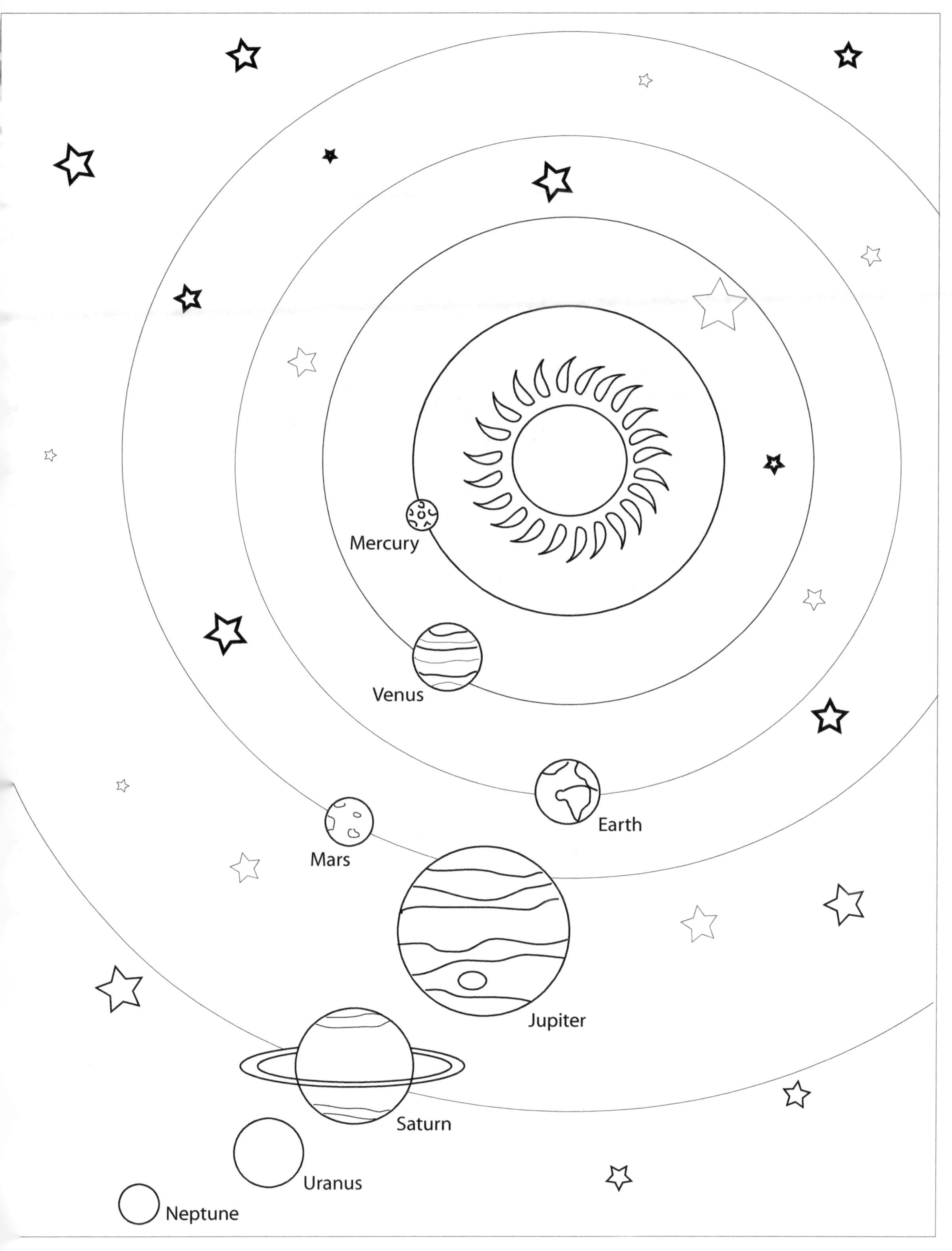

Mercury
Venus
Earth
Mars
Jupiter
Saturn
Uranus
Neptune

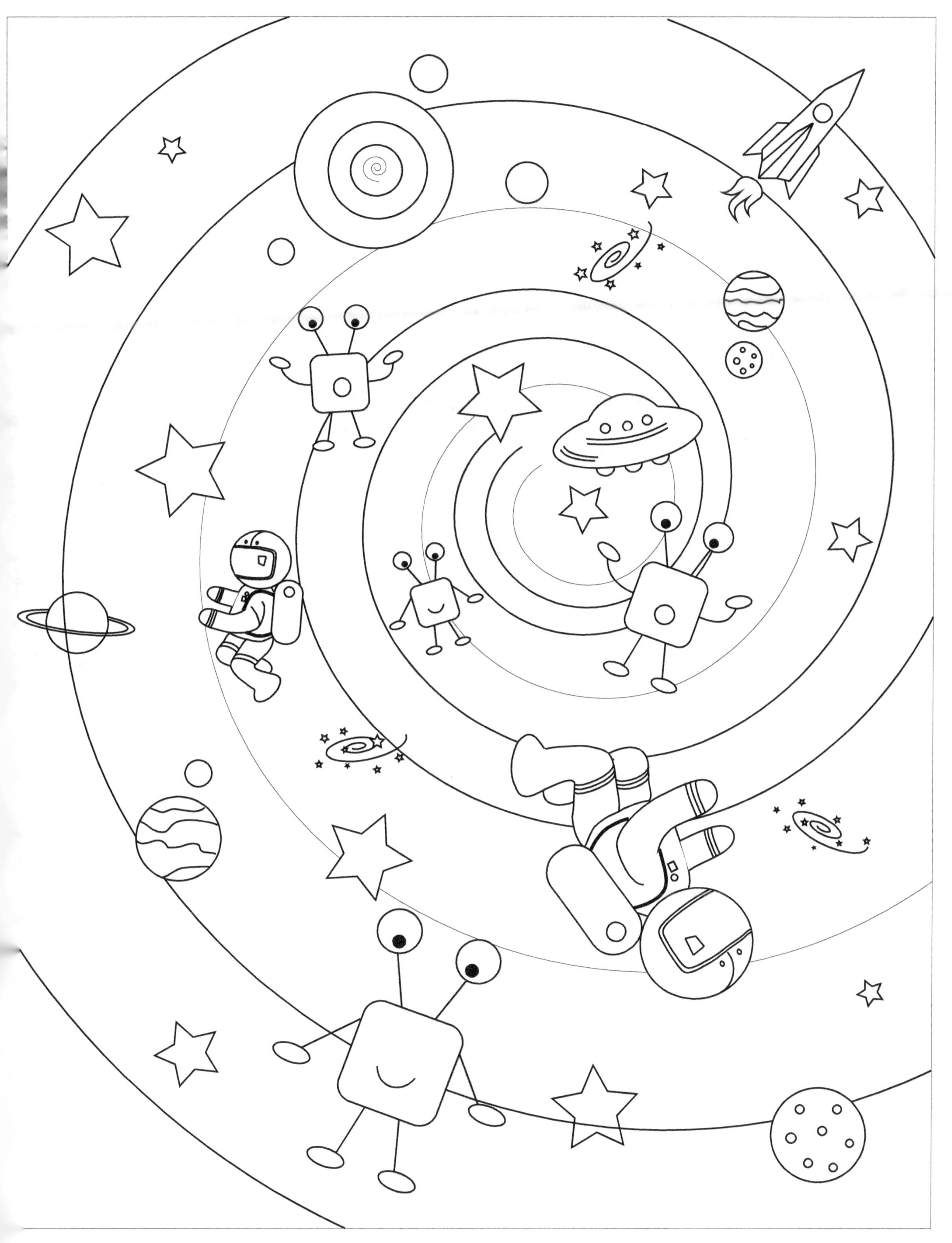

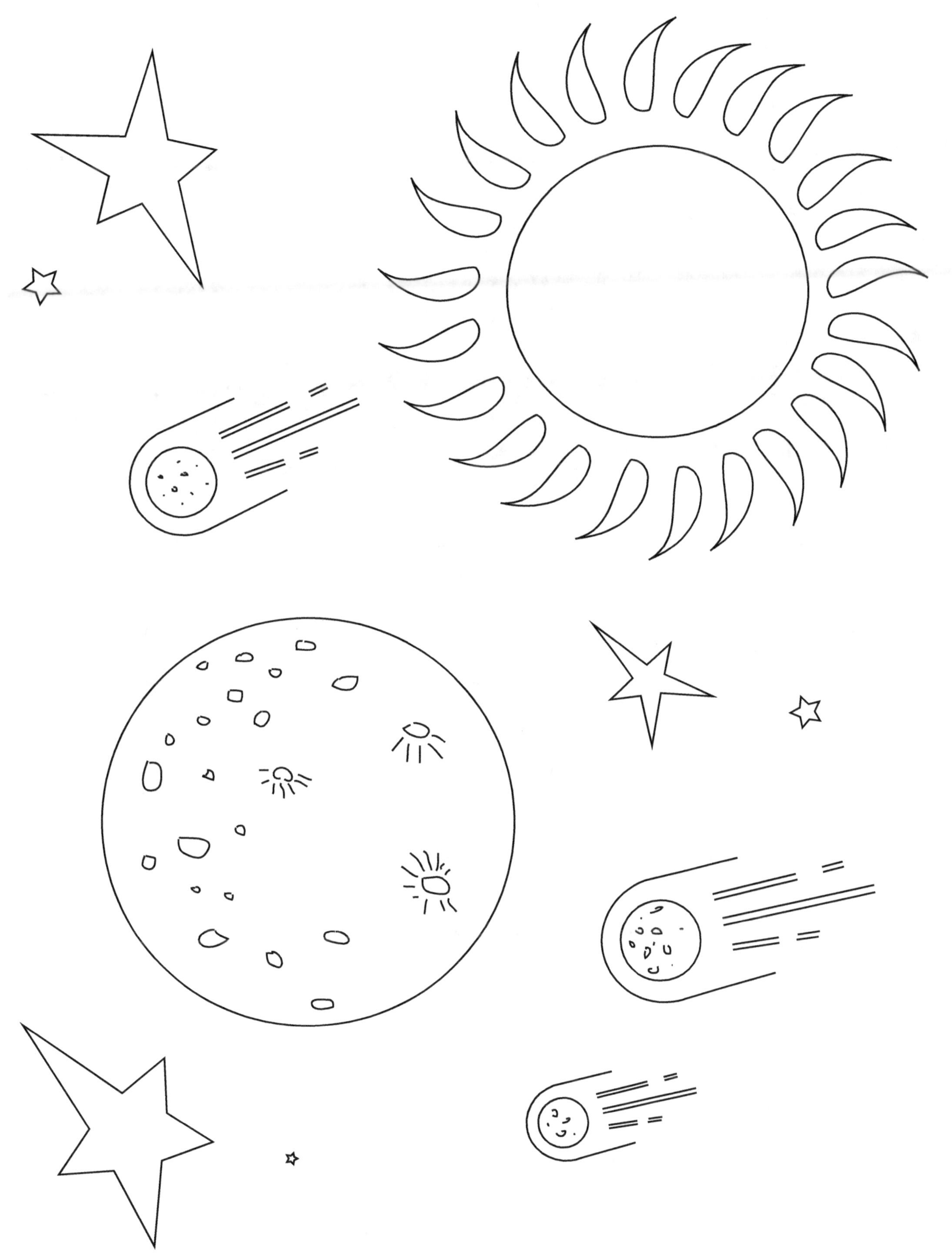

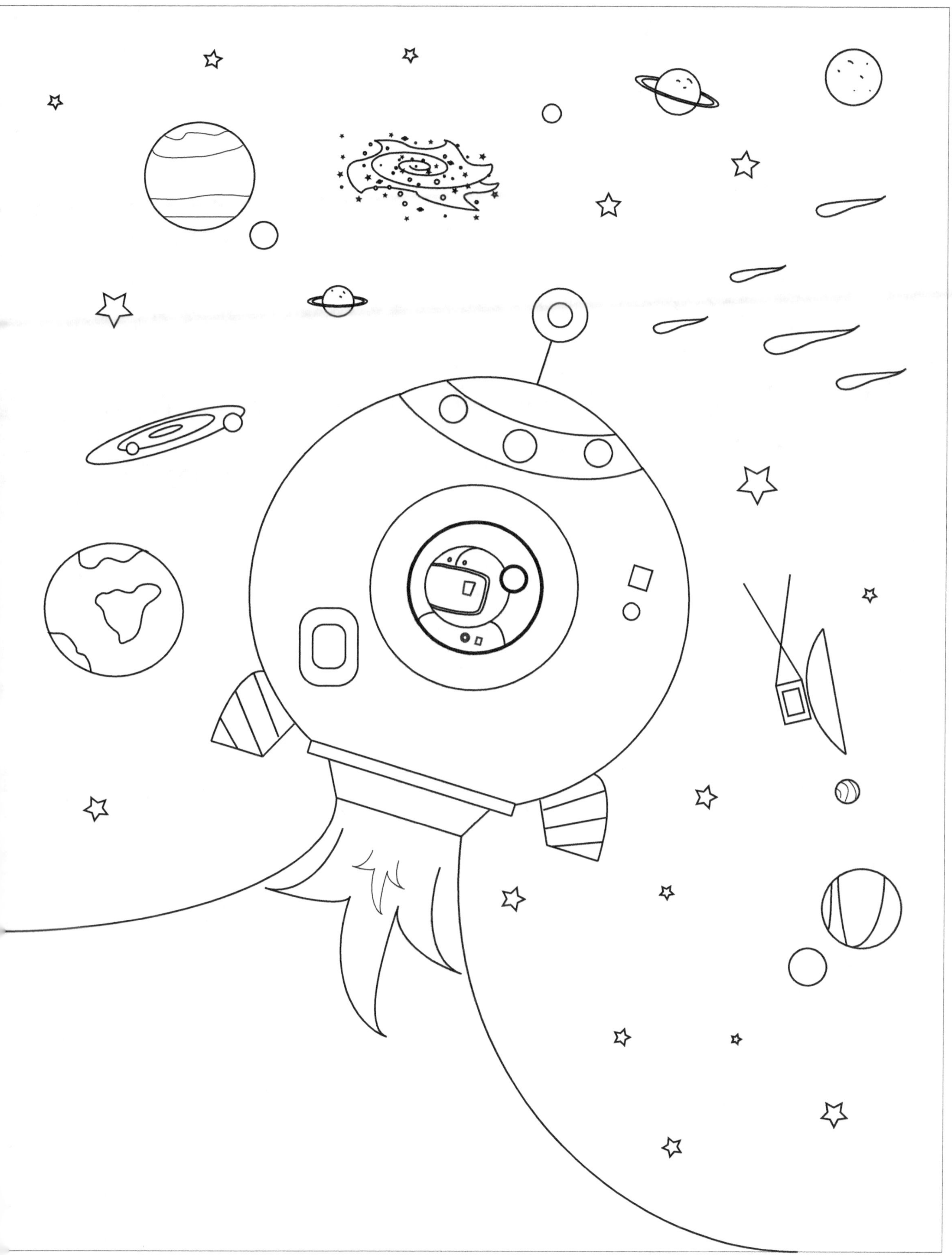

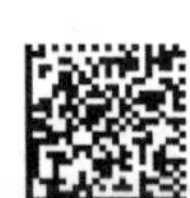

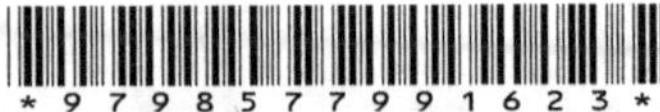
9 798577 991623